I0449697

PLANNING TO PREPARE, PREPARING THE PLAN

By

Q.M. Preston

Copyright © 2019 by Q. M. Preston

All rights reserved. No part of this publication may be reproduced, distributed, or transmitted in any form or by any means, including photocopying, recording, or other electronic or mechanical methods, without the prior written permission of the publisher, except in the case of brief quotations embodied in critical reviews and certain other noncommercial uses permitted by copywrite law. Purchasers of this book may print or photocopy blank forms and tables as needed for completing their own emergency plans.

Dedicated to all those working to keep friends and family safe in world of growing threats

Table of Contents

Foreword

Interest in planning and preparing for emergencies has grown exponentially in recent years. Blizzards, hurricanes, industrial accidents, and terrorist attacks are examples of events in the news that have inspired people to take steps to care for themselves. People from all walks of life are preparing for emergencies from relatively small power outages up to doomsday scenarios. When you first start to contemplate all the things that go into emergency readiness, you can quickly feel overwhelmed. I created this book to help reduce that stress and provide a path for achieving your own readiness.

This book is not designed to answer all your questions about prepping. In fact, this book is meant to ask *you* questions. It will then help you find the answers that work for you. If you consider all the individual specifics involved in preparing for emergencies, you soon realize that it is impossible to write a book that provides answers for every person.

Neither is it designed to give you plans for reacting to emergencies. My purpose here is to help you plan for getting to your starting point. Too often in the preparedness community, people develop a mindset of trying to get everything to prepare for everything. Do you really need to buy a huge property in the wilderness? Do you need a military-grade truck with solar panels and run-flat tires? Possibly. But why would you spend money on things that end up not helping you in emergencies you may face? Even more importantly, why spend money to solve a problem that could be solved with good planning and procedures?

To become truly prepared, you need to know your start point and your desired end point. When you have those, you need to develop your route. Just as looking at your desired destination on a map won't help you arrive, just knowing that you want to be ready for emergencies won't make you ready. You need to assess what your true needs are, determine your shortages, and develop your plan to eliminate those shortages. This includes shortages in supplies, equipment, and abilities. This plan needs to be specific to your circumstances, contain achievable goals, and needs to include specific steps within a timeline to achieve those goals.

My novel, Coming Together, in the Stronghold series, tells the fictional story of a family struggling to survive a cataclysmic emergency and is based very loosely on my family's plans. It addresses, in storytelling form, many of the concepts I will discuss here and expands upon them. This book is a workbook meant to help you follow the same path to develop your own plan.

While the procedures in this book are largely based on my years of training and experience with the military, I promise to keep the jargon to a minimum. I'll strive to keep everything as easy to understand as possible. My main desire is to help everyone find the easiest ways to better prepare themselves for emergencies. In each chapter, I will offer guidelines to consider, ask starter questions to get you thinking, and provide places to write your specific answers. At the end, I will provide contact information in case you desire further explanation.

By the time we finish this book together, you should have an initial plan for getting yourself and your family to a higher state of readiness. Keep in mind that the final plan is not meant to be unchangeable. Further reflection and changes in circumstances will lead to continuous refinements. I recommend you review the plan at least every three months. Now grab your pencils and calculators, get your family involved, and let's begin this journey together.

Chapter 1

What is Our Mission?

Determining your mission as an individual or family is the most crucial step in the process of developing your plan. You may think, "The mission is simple. Stay alive through any emergency." That's true in a general sense but it fails to capture several key elements. A complete mission statement is concise, clear, and captures the specifics of what you need to accomplish. Consider these two examples:

Example 1: Keep my family alive in any disaster.

Example 2: Maintain safety and sustainability of ten family and friends during hurricanes, tornadoes, and rampant civil unrest.

You can easily see that the second example establishes clear and specific goals. It creates good guidelines to direct your planning. The first example does not help in developing a specific plan. While some could say that it is better to plan for every possibility, focusing on likely threats will help avoid wasted time and resources. Is it necessary to plan for a major blizzard in central Florida or a hurricane in Nebraska? By developing a well-crafted mission statement, you can focus your valuable time and resources on the things you are most likely to face.

Let's begin developing your mission statement by looking at your specific who, what, where, and, to a certain extent, when. I'll ask some key questions and provide a list of possible answers with different degrees of likelihood to start you thinking. Then, I'll provide space for you to write in your own answers.

1. Who does the plan cover? List specific individuals by name. This will be helpful later. When writing the mission statement, just use the total number. (Husband, wife, significant other, parents, children, friends, other relatives)

_____

_____

_____

_____

2. Where are you living? If you are considering evacuating, what is your planned evacuation destination?

_____

_____

_____

3. What are the most likely natural emergencies you face? (Blizzards, earthquakes, tornadoes)

_____

_____

_____

_____

_____

_____

4. What are the most likely man-made emergencies you face? (Chemical spill, civil unrest, crime, terrorism, nuclear power plant accident)

_____

_____

_____

_____

_____

_____

5. If applicable, when could the emergency happen? (Winter begins in x months, hurricane season is in x months)

_____

_____

_____

_____

6. How long is the most severe emergency likely to last?

_____

_____

Keep in mind that some emergencies can coincide. The most obvious examples are looting during a hurricane or a chemical spill during a tornado. To help keep your mission statement simple, you do not need to address all the resultant emergencies. We will address those later. Focus on the major situations you anticipate.

Using your answers to the questions above, write your mission statement here. Be sure to use a pencil. You may decide to revise your statement as we progress.

_____

_____

_____

_____

_____

_____

Congratulations! You've completed the first crucial step in developing your plan. A clear, concise, and thorough mission statement will be the foundation of your plan. Keep it in mind as we progress through the remaining steps. You may even consider writing it out and hanging it somewhere that you can see it often. Frequently thinking about your mission will help you improve your plan over time. Now, let's move on to some more specifics.

Chapter 2

Who is with us?

Let's revisit the list of names you created in the last chapter. We're going to look at them in more detail. This is your core team. Your mission is to keep them safe, but each one will have a role to play in accomplishing that mission. You need to conduct an honest assessment of each person, including yourself. Identify skills they have, any medical conditions, other strengths and weaknesses, special needs or considerations, and training they need. This is also a good place to annotate at least two methods to contact each person. Use the table below as a guide. The first line is an example.

Name	Skills	Medical	Strengths	Weaknesses	Special Needs	Training	Contact Info
Jason	Planning Tactics Construction	Bad Knees	Communication Physically Fit Leadership	HAM operation Needs meds		HAM Food preservation	

Chapter 3

What do we need?

This will be the longest and most complex chapter of the book. We'll look at several categories of equipment and ask two questions. What do we have? What do we need to have? This will tell us what we still need to work on acquiring. When you think of all the supplies and equipment you could need in an emergency, it can become overwhelming. One thing that always helps me is to remember a riddle. How do you eat an elephant? One bite at a time. This is exactly how we'll address this chapter. We'll take it one step at a time, starting with equipment.

We start with equipment because the equipment you have and acquire will drive a lot of the supplies you will need to have on hand. To determine your equipment needs, you need to consider your mission statement. What emergencies do you anticipate? What will you be doing? For example, will you be sitting at home remaining mostly sedentary while riding out a tornado's aftermath? Or will you be traveling hundreds of miles to a remote area because you anticipate a total grid collapse? Also, keep in mind the number of people you will have with you. Does each person need a certain piece of equipment or can a few items be shared? Everyone will need a way to keep water with them, but several people can ride in one vehicle.

Over the next few pages, I have lists of equipment broken down by categories. I've included starter suggestions again and several blanks that you can fill in with your specific needs. When doing my own planning, I strive to include as many item as possible that serve multiple roles. One of my favorites is a strong pair of fencing pliers. These can serve many roles such as wire cutter, nail puller, hammer, small pry tool, and even a weapon if necessary. Several other items can also perform multiple functions. In determining quantities, I follow the philosophy of one is none and two is one. This means always have at least one spare.

Equipment

Required		On Hand		Need To Acquire	
Quantity	Item	Quantity	Item	Quantity	Item
Radios					
	Weather Alert				
	Handheld Two-way				
	HAM				

Required		On Hand		Need To Acquire	
Quantity	Item	Quantity	Item	Quantity	Item
Vehicles					
	4WD Pickup				
	Panel van				
	Mechanic tool kit				
	Tire repair kit				
	Spare gas cans				
	Generator				

Required		On Hand		Need To Acquire	
Quantity	Item	Quantity	Item	Quantity	Item
Weapons					
	Hunting Rifle				
	Shotgun				
	Pistol				
	Fixed blade knife				
	Knife sharpener				
	Weapon Cleaning Kit				

Required		On Hand		Need To Acquire	
Quantity	Item	Quantity	Item	Quantity	Item
Tools					
	Carpenter tool kit				
	Electrician tool kit				
	Plumbing tools				
	Garden tools				
	Chain Saw				

Required		On Hand		Need To Acquire	
Quantity	Item	Quantity	Item	Quantity	Item
Clothing and Individual Equipment					
	Shirts				
	Pants				
	Hats				
	Gloves				
	Canteen				
	Backpack				

Required		On Hand		Need To Acquire	
Quantity	Item	Quantity	Item	Quantity	Item
Miscellaneous Items					
	Water purification kit				
	Rain Barrel				
	Battery powered fan				
	Grill				

Supplies

That covers equipment for now. Remember, you may need to go back and make revisions as the plan progresses. Let's look at supplies. We have several questions we need to address up front before we get into specifics. Here are the questions to consider.

How many people? _____

What is the emergency? _____

What are we doing? (Sedentary or active)

_____

Are there medical conditions?

_____

How long will we be on our own?

_____

Are there special dietary conditions?

_____

Are there pets or domesticated animals to consider?

_____

What are our environmental conditions? (Hot, arid, cold, high rainfall)

_____

_____

_____

Other
Considerations_____

_____

_____

_____

_____

_____

_____

Food and Water

When planning for supply quantities, I always start with water and food as they are the most critical. For both, I start with a one week supply for each person and build up my quantities from there. Water will be dependent upon the type of environment you live in and the activity level you anticipate. I start with a two gallon per person per day planning factor. One gallon is for drinking and the other is to allow for hygiene and cooking. If you have the means to purify water and a way to reliably collect it, you can keep less on hand. I recommend always having at least one week's worth of purified water on hand as a minimum.

I break food into three categories for calculations. They are meats, starches, and fruits and vegetables. I plan based on three servings of meat, three of starches, and five of fruits and vegetables per person per day. When purchasing food supplies, keep serving sizes in mind. It may be possible to believe that one can of vegetables equals one serving. However, it could equal three. Also this is where dietary restrictions and preferences come into play. While it is true that in an extreme emergency there will be hardship and sacrifice, with good planning, you can minimize it. If you detest spinach, do not buy six cases of it just because the warehouse store has it on sale. If a member of your party is vegetarian, be sure to stockpile meat alternatives for them. Also, consider additional items that can help with morale such as chips, nuts, candies, or sodas.

Calculations:

Water _____ people x _____ gallons per day x _____ days = _____ gallons

Food

Meat (or substitute) ____ people x 3 per day x _____ days = _____ servings

Starches ____ people x 3 per day x _____ days = _____ servings

Fruits/ Vegetables ____ people x 5 per day x _____ days = _____ servings

Inventory List

Required		On Hand		Need To Acquire	
Quantity	Item	Quantity	Item	Quantity	Item
Water					
Meats					
Starches					

Required		On Hand		Need To Acquire	
Quantity	Item	Quantity	Item	Quantity	Item
Fruits					
Vegetables					
Other items (Snacks, cooking oils, spices, coffee, etc.)					

First Aid

The next priority is medication and first aid items. These will be based on your specific needs and anticipated situations. This will include any medications team members require, general first aid kits, and trauma supplies. Again, I've started some examples for you to consider.

Required		On Hand		Need To Acquire	
Quantity	Item	Quantity	Item	Quantity	Item
	Rubbing Alcohol				
	Hydrogen Peroxide				
	Gauze pads				
	Adhesive bandages				
	Ibuprofen				
	ACE Bandage				
	Clotting bandage				
	Suture Kit				

Required		On Hand		Need To Acquire	
Quantity	Item	Quantity	Item	Quantity	Item

Hygiene

Hygiene items are just as important as first aid items. Proper hygiene will help avoid most diseases and infections, reducing the need for medications. The most effective way I found to determine needed quantities is to track how often I empty soaps, shampoos, etc. over a period of three months. I then determine the average time that each item lasts.

Required		On Hand		Need To Acquire	
Quantity	Item	Quantity	Item	Quantity	Item
	Soap				
	Shampoo				
	Razors				
	Tampons				
	Feminine Pads				
	Toilet paper				
	Cleansing wipes				
	Deodorant				

Cleaning Supplies

Cleaning supplies are hygiene for your environment. This is another area where your planned activity will affect what you need. Brooms and mops will not be a priority if you plan on being on the move but are very important if staying home.

Required		On Hand		Need To Acquire	
Quantity	Item	Quantity	Item	Quantity	Item
	Bleach				
	Laundry detergent				
	Brooms				
	Paper towels				
	Floor cleaner				
	Cleaning rags				
	Disinfecting wipes				

Fuels and lubricants

Determining your fuel and lubricant needs is heavily dependent upon both your equipment we identified earlier in this chapter and your planned activity. While it covers needs for vehicles and generators, it also includes such things as fuel for grills (either charcoal or propane) and such things as spray lubricants and lubricants for weapons.

Required		On Hand		Need To Acquire	
Quantity	Item	Quantity	Item	Quantity	Item
	Gasoline				
	Motor oil				
	Grease				
	Spray lubricant				
	Gun cleaning solvent				
	Gun oil				
	Charcoal				
	Firewood				
	Charcoal starter				
	Solar chargers				

Ammunition

Your ammunition requirements will be based on the weapons you have now and plan to acquire plus your anticipated threats. Personally, I set an initial goal for each type of ammunition and then continue to build from there. When operating on a budget, I recommend buying small quantities of each needed type instead of buying large quantities of one type at a time.

Required		On Hand		Need To Acquire	
Quantity	Item	Quantity	Item	Quantity	Item
	.22 Long Rifle				
	12ga Slug				
	12ga Buckshot				
	9 mm				

Construction Materials and Hardware

Most of the items in this category may not be necessary if you don't plan to stay home during the emergency. However, some of them, such as duct tape, can be useful in many situations. Quantities needed will depend on the size of your home, number of windows and doors, etc. At a minimum, you want to be able to cover your windows and reinforce your doors. Fencing material, sandbags, and barbed wire can supplement your home security. You'll also need a good supply of a variety of nails, screws, and other hardware for maintaining your home. When considering what you need to barricade entrances, keep in mind that furniture and non-functioning major appliances can also be used.

Required		On Hand		Need To Acquire	
Quantity	Item	Quantity	Item	Quantity	Item
	¾" thick plywood				
	2"x4" lumber				
	2"x6" lumber				
	Sandbags				
	Barbed wire				
	16d Nails				
	8d nails				
	Plastic sheeting				
	Tarps				
	Electrical tape				
	PVC pipe				
	Pipe fittings				
	Vehicle repair parts				
	Weapon repair parts				

Miscellaneous and comfort items

This category covers things to help with physical comfort, morale, and anything not covered in the previous categories. Specific items and quantities are based on your specific needs and anticipated plans.

Required		On Hand		Need To Acquire	
Quantity	Item	Quantity	Item	Quantity	Item
	Blankets				
	Sleeping bags				
	Board Games				
	Card games				
	Books				
	Paper				
	Pens/Pencils				
	Alcohol				
	D cell batteries				
	AA batteries				
	AAA batteries				

Cash and Currency

Finally, we need to discuss cash. In almost every emergency you can imagine, there will be at least some period of time that debit and credit cards will be useless. Having cash on hand is always a good idea. Plus, remember to "keep the change", especially quarters. In some cases, laundry and vending machines may be operational before ATMs. If you are planning for long-term emergencies, you may want to consider having gold and silver bars and coins as well.

Required		On Hand		Need To Acquire	
Quantity	Item	Quantity	Item	Quantity	Item
Cash and Currency					
	Cash				
	Current coins				
	Silver coins				
	Silver bars				
	Gold coins				
	Gold bars				

Chapter 4

What is our current state? (SWOT Analysis)

We've almost completed our determination of where we are and where we want to go. We know that our desired destination is to be able to perform our mission statement. We know our existing environment, the people involved, and the supplies and equipment we have on hand. Now it's time to do our final analysis in order to fully define our current state.

To do this we use a tool called a SWOT analysis. SWOT stands for Strengths, Weaknesses, Opportunities, and Threats. It requires an honest and thorough evaluation of each person, your planned location, and your group as a whole. I'll discuss each element in turn and give you space to identify your own SWOT.

Strengths

You've already completed a part of this task earlier when you identified your team members. Take a look at that chart and identify some key strengths here. You don't have to list every strength for each individual here. Focus on things that support the overall mission. Also, look at characteristics of your team as a whole. Are they cohesive? Have they trained in different tasks together? Is the team large enough to adequately defend your home if necessary? Finally, look at your location and home. Is it sturdy? Do you have enough space to put in a garden? Is your weather conducive to collecting rainwater? Look at yourself, your individuals, your team, and your environment to identify everything that would be useful to surviving an emergency.

Strengths		
Individual	Team	Environment

Weaknesses

The next step is to evaluate your individuals, team, and environment again, this time identifying shortfalls and weaknesses. Be completely honest and objective. This exercise is not meant to criticize or degrade anyone. You are identifying potential problem areas so that you can later find ways to eliminate or accommodate them. For example, it is not a criticism of a person to state that they are not fit to complete an arduous hundred mile walk. It is simply a statement of fact. Once you are aware of it, you can act to prevent it from disrupting your mission.

Weaknesses		
Individual	Team	Environment

Opportunities

Opportunities are situations or conditions that exist now or during an emergency that work in your favor. If you are in a bad location, do you have the ability to relocate? Are you in a position where you can afford to increase your supply stockpiles? Do you have time each day to improve everyone's fitness level? In the event of an emergency, are there things or places around you that can aid your situation?

Opportunities		
Individual	Team	Environment

Threats

Threats include the emergencies for which you are preparing and any other external factors that could negatively impact your situation. The potential for extreme weather is a prime example. Do you live in an area with high gang activity? Could a lack of medical facilities endanger a team member with a medical condition?

Threats		
Individual	Team	Environment

Now that the SWOT analysis is complete you have a good picture of where your team stands in terms of being able to survive an emergency. You know your specific mission. You know your team members and their strengths and weaknesses. You know the supplies and equipment that you have on hand and what you need to acquire. Finally, you know the threats and opportunities that you face. With that knowledge, it's time to move to the next phase of the process, deciding the best course of action to take in the event of an emergency.

Chapter 5

Bug in or Bug out? (Determining Courses of Action)

This is the point where your plan may become a few sub-plans. As you analyze the courses of action for your anticipated emergencies, you may determine that the best course of action for one is to stay home and hunker down (bug in) but the best course for another is to evacuate to a safe area (bug out). Each option has advantages and disadvantages. You'll have to determine which works best for you. In some cases, it may be that you have no choice. A wildfire could force you to evacuate even if you had planned to never leave home.

The best method for determining your plan is to use a decision matrix. This is a tool that helps limit subjectivity and emotion from important decisions. It consists of establishing courses of action (COA) and identifying criteria to evaluate those courses. Numerical values are assigned to each course for all the criteria. The course with the highest score is the best answer to select. We'll walk through the steps together and build a matrix for an emergency. Again, I'll provide examples but leave room for you to enter your own specific answers.

Whenever possible, you should complete this exercise as a group. Every member of the team will have valuable input and can provide insights that a single person might not consider.

First, select one of the emergencies you identified in your mission statement and write it in the space at the top of the below table.

Emergency: (ex. Hurricane)			
Criteria / (Weight)	COA 1	COA 2	COA 3
Total			

The second step will involve the most intense critical thought on your part. Using your current status of supplies and equipment, your SWOT analysis, and what you know of the threat, you should develop two or three courses of action. You can often develop more than three, especially if you brainstorm as a group. To maximize the efficiency of the decision matrix, you should narrow your possibilities down to the three best. For the example of the hurricane, I selected remain home, evacuate inland, and evacuate to local shelter. Add your own courses to the table.

Emergency: (ex. Hurricane)			
Criteria / (Weight)	COA 1: Home	COA 2: Evacuate	COA 3: Local Shelter
Total			

Now that we have three courses of action to choose from, we need to establish criteria we want to use to evaluate the courses. These are items that apply to all three courses and are things you need to consider about them. Examples are considerations such as cost, risk, security, safety, and long-term sustainability. Select three or four items for your own situation. For the example, I chose safety, risk of travel, and security.

The next step is to assign relative weights to one or two criteria. Of the criteria you selected, is there one consideration that is more important than the others? Is there a second that is slightly less important than the first? We'll assign weights to those. For the example, I believe that safety is most important and security is second most. Since I have three criteria, I assign a weight of 3 to safety and 2 to security. This leaves risk of travel as a 1. This will be used in the next step. For now, list your criteria and weights in the table.

Emergency: (ex. Hurricane)			
Criteria / (Weight)	COA 1: Home	COA 2: Evacuate	COA 3: Local Shelter
Safety (3)			
Risk of Travel			
Security (2)			
Total			

The next step requires objective thought in evaluating the courses of action and assigning numerical values. Let's start by looking at the examples. When it comes to safety, I believe that a total evacuation is best, followed by local shelter, and staying home is worst. I would assign values of 3, 2, and 1 respectively.

Emergency: (ex. Hurricane)			
Criteria / (Weight)	COA 1: Home	COA 2: Evacuate	COA 3: Local Shelter
Safety (3)	1	3	2
Risk of Travel			
Security (2)			
Total			

But, remember that we assigned weights to the criteria in the previous step. This is when they come into play. We had assigned a weight of 3 to safety. Now, multiply each of the assigned values by 3 and add that into the table.

Emergency: (ex. Hurricane)			
Criteria / (Weight)	COA 1: Home	COA 2: Evacuate	COA 3: Local Shelter
Safety (3)	1 (3)	3 (9)	2 (6)
Risk of Travel			
Security (2)			
Total			

Complete those same steps for your remaining criteria. I've provided examples based upon my own thoughts. Your answers may differ.

Emergency: (ex. Hurricane)			
Criteria / (Weight)	COA 1: Home	COA 2: Evacuate	COA 3: Local Shelter
Safety (3)	1 (3)	3 (9)	2 (6)
Risk of Travel	3 (3)	1 (1)	2 (2)
Security (2)	3 (6)	1 (1)	2 (4)
Total			

The final step is to total the assigned values to determine the best course of action. Remember to use the values that are in the parentheses. The course of action with the highest total is the best solution based upon the criteria you determined is important to you.

Emergency: (ex. Hurricane)			
Criteria / (Weight)	COA 1: Home	COA 2: Evacuate	COA 3: Local Shelter
Safety (3)	1 (3)	3 (9)	2 (6)
Risk of Travel (1)	3 (3)	1 (1)	2 (2)
Security (2)	2 (4)	1 (1)	3 (6)
Total	10	11	14

Chapter 6

How Will We Achieve Readiness?

(Lines of Effort, Action Steps)

The time has come to lay out your plan to get to your desired end state in terms of training, supplies, and equipment. We're going to create your actual roadmap to get you from your current point to your destination.

I think of this as a strategic plan. It's an overarching plan for achieving readiness, not a specific plan to conduct an operation. Your strategic plan is going to consist of three key elements. We'll discuss each one and then build the plan.

Lines of effort

You should develop three to five lines of effort. These are broad categories that support reaching your desired end state. These could be areas such as fitness, supply acquisition, home improvement, etc.

Action Steps

These are specific steps taken to support the line of effort. They should always be well-defined and include the person responsible for completing the step. The steps should progressively build toward achieving the end state.

Timeline

You should always develop a realistic, achievable timeline for your plan.

The diagram on the next page is an example of a strategic plan that incorporates all the elements above. To diagram your own plan, you will need a larger sheet of paper or several pages pieced together.

Mission:

2019			2020
May	Aug	Dec	Jan

LOE 1: Improve Fitness

Jason enroll at gym	Jason complete 5K	Nancy complete Iron Man

LOE 2: Get needed supplies

Adam purchase new rifle	Jason purchase 72 hour food kit

LOE 3: Locate and move to new home

Jason find new job	Sarah locate property

Chapter 7

The N-Hour Sequence

You are now on your way to effectively preparing for emergency situations that you may face. Before we end our time together, I want to offer you one more tool that could be useful, the N-Hour sequence. This planning tool is designed for when the emergency happens or is imminent. It lists specific tasks and times for them to be completed in relation to initiating the plan. It includes time, activity, responsible party, and location if applicable. You will want to create an N-hour sequence for each emergency you might face. I'll provide some examples in the first few line of the table to get you started.

Time	Activity	Person	Location
N	Notification of emergency		
N+5 minutes	Begin boarding windows	Jason	
N+5 minutes	Begin filling water containers	Sarah	
N+30 minutes	Begin loading weapon magazines	Sarah	
N+2 hours	Put out barbed wire	Jason	
N+3 hours	Prepare battery powered lights	Sarah	
N+ 1 day	Begin filling sand bags	Jason	

Time	Activity	Person	Location

About the author:

Q.M. Preston is the pseudonym for an author currently residing in the southern U.S. He has over twenty years of experience in the U.S. military in numerous roles, primarily in logistics and planning. His entire adult life has been spent studying and applying principles of emergency preparedness. He draws upon his professional experiences in planning for major events and certain aspects of his own family's plan to aid others in developing their plans. He intends for his books to be entertaining but also serve as training manuals for preparedness-minded individuals from the novice to the expert.

If you have questions or would like more information, you can contact him by email at qmpreston@qmpreston.com, by visiting qmpreston.com, or by following him on Facebook and Twitter.

www.ingramcontent.com/pod-product-compliance
Lightning Source LLC
Chambersburg PA
CBHW081604280526

45788CB00011B/3546